in case of emergency press

We are proud to acknowledge the Traditional Owners of country throughout Australia and to recognise their continuing connection to land, waters, and culture. We pay our respects to their Elders.

We support recognition, reconciliation, and reparation.

Let the Baby Sleep

Patrick T. Reardon

in case of emergency press
https://icoe.com.au
Travancore, Victoria
Australia

Published by in case of emergency press 2023

Copyright © Patrick T. Reardon 2023

All rights reserved. Without limiting the rights under copyright reserved above, no part of this publication may be reproduced, stored in or introduced into a database and retrieval system or transmitted in any form or any means (electronic, mechanical, photocopying, recording or otherwise) without the prior written permission of both the owner of copyright and the publisher.

ISBN: 978-0-6458496-3-9

Cover design: Ward Nikriph

Photograph of 13th Century stained glass used by permission, Chartres Cathedral, France

Acknowledgements

Thanks to these publications where these poems or an earlier version initially appeared:

After Hours: "Lament"
Beyond Words: "Package goods"
Bindweed: "Against Consolation," "David in the Rain" and "In the Other Room"
Bold Monkey: "Enough to Be on Your Way" and "The Problem of Human Suffering"
Burningword Literary Journal: "Let me tell you"
Digging Through the Fat: "How"
Down in the Dirt: "My brother's afflictions and mine," "Salome" and "Teach"
Drunk Monkeys: "A reading from the Book of My Brother"
Esthetic Apostle: "She broke"
Ground Fresh Thursday: "Let Us Now" (as "She grabbed the pigeon")
Jabber: "Same" and "The cloud of every thing"
Literary Orphans: "Four percent pantomime"
Main Street Rag: "Workingman's blues #7"
Outlaw Poetry: "Absent angel"
Poetry Quarterly: "When she's gone, she's gone"
Pump Don't Work: "...ad altari Dei"
Rat's Ass Review: "When"
San Antonio Review: "Audrey in Confession"
Silver Birch Press: "Finding pain," "Saw you at the hop" and "Sugar Jets"
The Write Launch: "Baby"
Tipton Poetry: "Lot's brother"
UCity Review: "Go"
Write City: "It Makes No Difference"

Dedicated to my sweet brother, David

As always, for Cathy, and Sarah and John and Ulysses and David and Tara and Emmaline and Noah.

Thanks to Thomas Pace, Julie Coplon and Joan Servatius.

Table of Contents

I am in need of comfort 1
    She broke 3
    Saw you at the hop 5
    Audrey in Confession 7
    Fashioning 8
    Jericho woman 9
    The bliss of his oblivion 12
    Against consolation 15
    Same 17
    Interrogatories 18
    David in the rain 20
    Bird 21
    Go 22

Foreign ourselves 27
    When 29
    Every thing on the earth 31
    Unearthed 33
    Lovingkindness 35
    Baby 37
    Teach 38
    Jim E. Lee 39
    Steel sharp 41
    That nervous one 43
    The cloud of every thing 44

Never delivered 47
    Package goods 49
    Four percent pantomime 50
    When she's gone, she's gone 51
    In the other room 52
    Absent angel 53
    Lot's brother 54
    How 55

Lectionary	57
A reading from the Book of My Brother	58
Apparitions	59
…ad altare Dei	61
Salome	62
Soon enough	**63**
Magnificat	65
The problem of human suffering	66
It makes no difference	67
Finding pain	68
Real real gone	70
Shards	71
Sugar Jets	73
Lament	74
Swing	77
Buried her ashes	78
My brother's afflictions and mine	80
Workingman's blues #7	81
Let us now	82
Enough to be on your way	83
Steps	85
Let me tell you	87
About the Author	**91**

Let the Baby Sleep

Patrick T. Reardon

"... the maidenliest star in the firmament twinkled..."
Edmund, *King Lear*, Act 1, Scene 2

I am in need of comfort

She broke

She broke my arm when I was a baby.
It wasn't my arm but call it an arm.
It mended crooked, at an odd angle,
thickened, clotted, stiff instead of supple,
a wrinkled butterfly wing, an antelope limp.
I could not swing a baseball bat
or brush a lover's hair.
I still have the broken arm.

My brother's hurt was worse. He died of it.

She tattooed her scripture on my spine, her
gospel proclamations on the inside of my
skull, her dire psalms on the bottom of my
right heel, on the sweep of my right hip,
black etched lines, leaking, insinuating.

> The tree grows out of my
> chest, another from my
> forearm, my jaw, my
> left shin. Syrup tapped,
> dripped, fermented, sold,
> re-sold. A forest where
> Abel kills, Noah drowns,
> the Messiah leper never
> gets the ghost back.

Let me open the apartment door of her
limping mother in the kitchen, baking
bread, breaking bread, the afternoon
sun jeweling soil and backyard dung

and growing things and creeping things
and the newborn and the dying and the
dead. Her bread was sprinkled with flour.

Two candles under a throat to bless away.

My brother used a nickel-plated
revolver instead, a blessing of
the endless white.

>   He was a wall
>   of alternating
>   anger and pain.
>   You try to live in that home.

He wanted to stomp-dance
on the harridan nun's grave.
Now, with his somber bullet,
his ashes are curb muck, roof
dust, grit in the hop-skip girl's
hair scattered in the wind.
No dancing on his grave for
anyone who hated him or loved.

Let the Baby Sleep

Saw you at the hop

I was nine when I saw
you through open
eighth grade door—
before you went to
Army, to Europe, to
Normandy Beach a
week after D-Day,
and hernia, and
British nurse Betsie,
and Germany, the camp.

Later, a man at the
Thomist Club dance
in school basement—
what was that year?—
your head close to
low ceiling, thin, solid,
arms akimbo.

I told you to dance
with me. Your eyes
dived into my brain
and neck and lungs
and chest and heart
and stomach and dark
place, full of light.

I am your island,
you, my fortress.
We close our front
door around each

other, over us, like
a counterpane, and
I am persuaded
that neither debt nor
wealth, nor demons,
nor powers, nor
tempting, nor
weaknesses, nor
now, nor future,
nor then, nor
height, nor depth,
nor width, nor sons
nor daughters in
their wildernesses,
nor all, nor nothing,
shall separate us.
We are enough.

Audrey in Confession

Bless me, Father. I can't conceive.
I am barren as gum-spotted sidewalk cement.

Forlorn in my failure to transubstantiate cells.

Wombed guilty in my shadow-shivering,
wombed empty, unquickened,
wombed naked in the gold and flame sanctuary,
wombed at the stake in the grit, dirt square.

I am sinful in my innocence,
wombed transgression,
wombed stain uncleansed,
wombed sweat and blood and semen soiled.

Wombed heartily.

In the pew
Hail Mary full
wash me whiter than snow.

Dream the tall policeman.

Fashioning

In the Book of Lost and Found, I read
David put Uriah on the front line
to find his death to free his wife
for David's bed.

In the Book of Majestic Resources, I read
Peter shook his head thrice, heard rooster cries,
alleluias to the lamb God, and
sorrowed past Judas at rope's end.

In the Book of Ashes and Stone, I read
Augustine wanted pure salvation eventually.

In the Book of Jo-Jo, I read
timid wife and husband
circumscribed days
to avoid danger of crossing the
line into right and wrong, delight and
exquisite sorrow, fashioning
a wall with the fragile lives of children.

Jericho woman

Jericho woman, waiting as
husband pumped car with
gas, looked at laundromat, as
if a space capsule.

Jericho woman thought of
her favorite nun every time
she found an answer.

First baby flummoxed Jericho
woman, nervoused, anxietied
skin on arms, pores on face.
Crying had to be controlled, the
crying, the crying. She had no
lips for fresh skin. No arms to
hold, except at arm's length, as
if he stank.

Jericho woman wouldn't learn
to drive. Every piece of mail,
Jericho woman burned. She could
not abide the sound of wind, said
it was souls in hell, groaning sour
pain.

Still water unsettled Jericho
woman. So, too, an uncornered
pile of papers, birds, animals of
any sort, requirements, gaps, as
if her soul might depart unbidden.

Giving birth was a task Jericho
woman understood. It was a clear
yes-no. In between times, she was
unpregnant with unclear lines. Each
many quickening of her womb was a
cubicle in a vast room, and each live
product a resident of that cubicle, as
if another brick in the wall.

Jericho woman was sane, south by
southwest. The forehead of each living
quickening was stamped with imprint
of her foot, a heel stone, as her heart
was stamped with mysterious rot and
her gray lungs with the breath of brick
dust.

Jericho woman ashed herself from
within. Withered inside out. Joyed
to beat death and burial costs by
giving body to science, a desiccated
donation to thick-blooded future
doctors and then was ashed again as
if twice blessed or
cursed or
certained.

Each night, for an hour, Jericho
woman would wake and worry,
smoking Pall Malls and plotting
her trip through the coming day,
through the heavy work of keeping
house walls up, the small bodies
fed, clothed and silent, as
if she would fracture at a word.

Jericho woman was careful not
to think of her father. Making a
mistake and dead brown leaves
on the curb line edge could not be
considered.

Jericho woman rearranged
furniture again as
if exorcising demons.

The bliss of his oblivion

Look at his drained body,
hair combed just-so to cover the hole.

Hear my brother's stutter.
He looked at me as if I could explain.

His Christmas arm across my shoulder,
anger pause,
then commence firing screaming shells
from clustered cruiser guns in a battle
to crush my peaceful nation, surrogate
for the argument with our mother he
could never win, she not risk losing.

Look through the telescope at the hint of his planet.
He inhabited his football uniform like for a moon-landing,
ordered milk in a bar,
read the on-off switch for answers.

His much-washed white t-shirt,
the bird-specked crabapple he ate on a dare,
his knowing that, if he asked, he would not be told.

He believed in worded pages that promised formulae,
never found his lost name,
mumbled Latin with me amid the altar incense,
a boy of stolid sorrows.

He rode into the dry sea with the other charioteers
and watched the water walls collapse,
a huge fluid stone,
on him, innocent Egyptian.

Let the Baby Sleep

They took a sledge and slammed his knees
so his cross could be stripped before sundown,
to keep holy the Sabbath.

He lived in his unwashed feet,
his lack of a wedding garment,
his spilled chalice,
his infestation of demons,
his transfiguration
at his back door in 3 AM rain-snow
with a gun more silver than all the stars,
in his blood tears,
in his wide-eyed slaughter,
in his Isaac moment
—God, bless the child—
no ram nearby, no arriving angel,
his arkless flood,
his hair shorn,
his third-degreed skin from the burning bush.

He wrestled with the angel and the sky opened
and the voice refused to say
anything about his son.

I found the lost tribes
after David's suicide,
before his First Communion,
during his betrayal,
under his sign at the end of the rainbow,
through his intercession,
before his relic,
within his boy's embrace,
beyond his blue horizon,
over his troubled crib,

on his feast day,
on his first day,
in his fragile voice in the final call,
not for help, for hearing, his Amen.

The applause he never heard.
The bliss of his oblivion.
His ashed body from the furnace.

He found no preacher at the Samaritan well
with eternal water
or any.

Against consolation

I do not see
you when the
street shouts
with light at
dawn. Not
hear you in
the clockwork
thunderstorm,
no drug for my
pain.

You do not talk
to me since that
night before your
gun. You never
whistled a happy
tune.

Did you see
that moon of
tonight on the
3 AM when
you moved out
into incautious
rain-snow? You
were taking your
first step past
caution. Gave
yourself no 2ND
step.

I am unconsoled.
Fine. Why expect
consolation? Just
another drug that
doesn't work. You
fingered your own
consolation. It
worked.

Same

It's the same moon Chaucer knew the rising of. It's the same lake Daniel Burnham saw as living water, ever in motion. It's the same corner where two grade-school brothers stood for an Easter photograph, and I am now alone alive. It's the same bullet he apologized for, as taught, that coursed an explosion through his brain. It's the same Mother's Day, and I am happy still she too is dead.

Interrogatories

Is child too unneedy to yearn connection?
Is dust of ash worthy soil?
Am I worthy?

Can betrayal be bleached away in the washer?
Is fear too tender for her to enunciate?
Why should I sacrifice on the altar stone?

   Item: Odin hanged himself on the World Tree branch.

Can I bear the botched translation of my song?
Is crone of death my bride?
Is bone picked bare by ravens sacred?

Will I evaporate like morning mist?
Can my empty fill?
Can my electricity arc?

   Item: The shark in utero cannibalized his brother.

Are we alone?
What means horse skull found in mine?
What means these bed stains?

Is my steel dented?
Has the gold of the doors worn away?
Am I on television?

   Item: Many animals depend upon mistletoe for food.

Let the Baby Sleep

Is there no map without these dark hells?
I wrestle at the foot of the ladder to nowhere.
Will my skin slough off to reveal beating heart?

Can my urgency survive?
Will Friend Chaos intrude?
Can child forgive?

David in the rain

Unlearn nun lesson.
Trample her grave. No joy.

Unfeel shoulder grip.
Twist neck, twist neck, muscle twitch.

Unclose eighth-grade eyes.
Unclose infant eyes, grandfather eyes.

Unvintage toxin.
Unkneel.

Unwrite tiny letters
on brick in chimney shadow.

Unscald skull.
Unchar heart.

Unwrite scripture.

Unhistory decades.
Unrestrain weeping.

Unopen gun drawer.
Unopen back door.

Unstand in thick snow-rain dark.
Unsteel.
Unpull.

Bird

Infant bird, barrel-chested, speckle-chested,
dark-splats against dirty coffee chest, skip-hops
along top of roll-up back porch sun screen
we haven't rolled up or down or thought of
as, unnoticed, bird mother architectured
stick-twig-ribbon nest at far right of roll-up top,
next to wood column, rust painted, safe harbor,
squared away from predators, and, in time,
swooped to feed three urgent beaks, but no
beaks today, only this one ship-hopping to and
fro along top of roll-up, others gone, flying—I
check cement below, unbodied—or predatored,
I guess, not here, only this one skip-hopping and
che-upping randomly, like rain drips after storm
or in pause before resumption, while mother
flies back and back and back distractedly, not
to feed beaks, but urging—what do I know?—
this one to flight although to my eyes the
brown-black wings seem too short to work,
and there is a low, tense startlement to the
eyes, circled in white, black as the cosmos,
skip-hopping now along the roll-up top to
the nest, standing tall, grooming, waiting, I
guess. What do I know?

Go

*In remembrance of Maggie Roche, Ben Scheinkopf,
George Kresovich and David Reardon*

Right onto Cermak from Harlem
to go west, listening
to the dead singer's song from
when she was young, from
when I was young
when I first heard it.

Manuscripts are completed with
no chance to edit.
END.

Left onto Mannheim,
the intersection I drove through
on the way back
to the Notre Dame girl's family
when I was young, untouched,
when she was young,
when we never knew each other,
not then or now,
our parents, childhood friends,
the intersection George and I
drove through on the way
to go to the barbecue,
when we were young and
George was alive,
singing together "Twist and Shout"
with the Beatles
when they were young
and all of them alive.

Let the Baby Sleep

At the McDonald's,
just before the tracks,
on the way to the table
where one sister and two brothers wait,
each old now, even the baby
who was born in the years
when I first heard the dead singer's song
with her sister
about a guy named George
who could go for her,
seductive reasoning.

   I could have gone for her.

South on California from Evanston,
past the barber shop
where Ben, out of Auschwitz,
cut my hair the last time
when he was 97, died
when he was 98,
his wife Emily talking still
—let my people go—
and I remember interviewing him
about Mayor Harold Washington,
dodging smashing-hate for a second term,
when I still worked for the *Tribune*,
when Ben was more than forty years
from the camp
where everyone in his family
had to go to be slain
except a brother (they shared bread)
who went to Israel later,
and Ben's touch was gentle,
in his fingers, I was the skull of someone
who would die, caressed.

Inside the mother whale, he
was trapped, swallowed,
lodged. She was a small
whale. He was crammed,
muscled up against her
fervid spleen, contracted
there even more when
she gave her ghost up,
and, years later, pain too
great, he cut his way out
to sea depths where he
drowned in freedom.

Near the table
where two brothers and a sister met me,
the short woman
among the many short restaurant workers,
looking up, asked me if I had been taller
when I was younger,
and I claimed, not knowing,
that I had not lost any height
when I was now getting to
the end of my sixties
because of basketball
and the chiropractor stretching me,
jarringly popping my back,
when each visit was near its end,
and she smiled, her eyes to mine,
a companion in the years and the world,
and I complimented her on the restaurant art,
envious of her family there
—all the workers of the same blood
or from the same village—
and turned to go back
to my superficial table.

> The father swaggered his petty kingdom,
> looking neither right nor left
> for fear.

Down West End toward Leamington
on the recess playground street,
yellow-paint wood police horses,
where I ran for the long pass
into John Reiter's teeth,
scalp sliced, both bleeding
as the nuns called,
blood dripped on the way to the office
on the Blacktop,
bleached gray by wear and sun,
where cars parked Sundays,
where tall boys played basketball,
where we would go to play slapball
(closed fist onto solid rubber ball)
and slide into base
in our gray work pants
on the gray asphalt
getting tiny stars of broken glass
embedded in the skin of our hands,
that, mornings, sparkled,
white, green and brown,
in the slant sun,
a constellation of city grit to awe Solomon

> Carved into the roof of the sky, words
> of sacred wind spinning since the world began
> and, in the whirl, listen to the human howl.

North on Tulley
past the house my brother lived
where I wouldn't go—after—to the back

where the sound of his self shot rippled
the air thick with rain snow,
where his brain blood stained
the sidewalk and grass,
hosed off, sacredly,
by a nephew and a brother-in-law,
priests of our sad song,
family at the world's wide table.

    The brother voted with his gun.
    He marked his ballot with a bullet hole
    and his blood on the backyard lawn.

Foreign ourselves

When

When I sit and when I stand.
When clots of fog cover the restless river.
When tick tocks.
When I die and when I am.

    (When inert bullet left and
    channeled his brain and spilled
    onto rain-snow concrete and grass,
    gray tissue and blood
    and his empty body.)

When Johnny comes
marching, when Irish
eyes, when the swallows
and when a man loves.

When ignorant armies.

When lake and river merge.
When sky and water merge.
When flesh scabs.
When hot flesh unites.
When flesh rots dry.

    (When his strobe anger lightninged a
    whirlwind upon me, his fellow prisoner
    in chains reaching back to the crib.)

When the red, red robin and
when doves. When the ship and
when I was a boy.

When I swallowed my unsung song.

When Jesus wept.
·When Judas kissed.
When Peter heard.

    (When he stuttered, when he learned
    poison lessons he couldn't vomit, when
    his leg was broken, but not his leg.)

When I, when we were, when the
saints, when the moon hits your
eye, when you wish, when you're
smiling, when you went away, when
you went away.

Every thing on the earth

She walked Red Sea Boulevard to the lake.

Walked past graystones and brownstones,
regal bungalows, two-flats, squat worker cottages,
past wall-like U-shaped apartment buildings,
sheening high-rises, dollar stores, laundromats,
past old mansions hived into clumsy kitchenettes,
sad Dunkin Donuts, the dress shop for quinceañeras.

In Toledo, he stole Gideon Bible from a Hyatt,
and put it in a bedroom dresser drawer.
Next time he looked, it was Gideon Koran.

Each night, he'd look and it was something different—
Gideon Book of Mormon, Gideon Bhagavad Gita,
Gideon Baseball Encyclopedia, Gideon OED,
Gideon Pride and Prejudice.

In blare-light dawn, she walked Red Sea Boulevard.

Along empty sidewalk,
uneven from soil heavings, root thrustings,
she walked, tiring as miles added up.
Along city wall, along shoreline wall, she walked.
Through clouds of birdsong.

He was alive only certain hours of the day.
Awoke at 11:14 AM from his stasis on the pedestal
and moved around until 7:39 PM
when he'd better be back on the stand or
it'd be embarrassing and uncomfortable.

He museumed his thoughts into
categories and schools, into
media, into pastels and etchings, into
the gift shop.

They met over Diet Cokes at cathedral McDonald's.
Prayed together over French fries.
Sang together in the booth thanksgiving canticle:

> *Sun and moon! Stars of heaven!*
> *Showers and dews! Winds! Fire and heat!*
> *Dews and sleet! Light and darkness!.*
> *Lightning and clouds! Mountains and hills!*
> *Every thing on the earth and in*
> *the air and under the earth, every thing that*
> *has been and will be!*
> *Bless!*

They bowed their heads toward each other,
foreheads touching over the table,
skin-to-skin kiss.

Then, he had to leave. It was after 7.

She sat, garnering her strength.
Then, she had to walk to get where she was going.

I looked up to see her leave.
Then, went back to *Don't Cry, Scream*.

Unearthed

He unearthed himself
with the tunnel through the brain,
carved with steel,
straight and smooth,
out of the barrel—
a scream that began when, one,
he stood at crib bars in pain, rage,
unprotected by me flat-face behind him, two.
God, bless the child.

He unearthed his bile,
torrent of hammer words,
expiation for someone's sins.

On that night,
he unearthed to me, frail,
the bone pain,
the joint pain,
the lines of pain that wrote his history,
unable to track back, forbidden,
alone at the end of the reaches,
desolate, before, hours later,
wrenching the
ever-sharpening,
stabbing
nerve endings
out his back door, calling
intention to 911,
and, then,
his perfect act.

Unearth his blood stream in the grass,
behind the home now owned by others,
unknowing of the soil's nutrients,
my brother's molecules,
atoms,
fluids and
matter,
unburnt in the funereal flames,
uncasketted,
unearthed
only in the green soft blades,
themselves bladed by the mower,
as my brother was
and I will be,
mulch for other earth.

Lovingkindness

I lost the bag of lovingkindness
on the bus—set it down, got up
at stop, pushed door, stepped
to curb, and, realized five steps
later, I was on a wind-etched
plateau empty-handed, bag
stolen or forgotten, lack of cloud
cover to the ends of the earth,
and a flock of righteousness
rejoiced, heading north, not
cartoon joy, shrill elation. The
headdress of hope the Halloween
Indian wore was in the clean-city
trash web after he was doused
with a gallon of shame-on-ice by
party host, and stopped homebound
for a glass of caress and a bowl of
ivory whims. Hope is that feathered-
shat, hard-shell seed in glaciered-
stone crevice. The infant knows,
each morning, explosion of opened
eyes until, older, explained away.
Keep lovingkindness in the clean
ashtray of petrified wood, blue.
Keep yearning in a breast heart-
beat pocket. Counsel is tall. Good
counsel is melodious. I taped my
refuge on my wall. My salvation I
honored with prime placement. I
breathed deep the intimate whirlwind
of belief. I drank my tea of love. At

line's end, final rider looked in bag,
took lovingkindness to the Jewel
Food Store loading dock, put it in an
empty trailer on its wayward way to
Merrionette Park, shrine of prophecy
and garden of earthly streetlights.

Baby

My sister held the baby as he died.
Not hers.

She held the nose-tube baby
as his mother exercised at the Y,
exorcized, for moments, grief,
setting fragile, ebbing boy in soft arms.

She came away from her office desk to help
and held the baby like her own,
embraced gently under a smile.

She held the baby as he died,
body and blood, chalice,
incense cloud, censer,
sacred fire.

She held the baby,
tied to him for final breathing,
son now, blessed in her living.

She held the baby as he died.
Hers.

Teach

Teach the baby his fault.
Teach the baby his distance.
His strap-down.
His adoration rubric.
His fool-ness.

    This is to protect you.

Read the baby the dread gospel,
chapter and verse of tattooed tension.
Roughen his skin with comical caustic.
Break his arm, his ankle.
Him tame.

    He is refuge from your danger.

Teach the ones that follow.
Enlist him to teach their fool-ness.
Enlist him to mortar them into refuge walls.

    Deny everything.

Write "Father of the Year" for the papers,
strut parents of the year in the pews.
After all, fourteen.

    No one will believe him.

Spotlight weight of numbers,
congregants at your altar.
After all, the poor mother.

    But, first, teach the baby his fault.

Jim E. Lee

Jim E. Lee, dopey with hope,
walking his haunted house
—not bright enough or too bright maybe—
past his brother's gun room,
past his mother's fear altar,
past his own caches of fear,
treasured like a never-healing wound,
proof of life, like the high church emptiness,
like the glimmer of gold, the incense bite.

Jim E. Lee feels the trick of the music,
of the won't-take-no-for-an-answer sunlight
through plate glass window
and onto the table
and along the fence,
wet, wilted leaves of cold autumn scripture,
the writing of a hand upon the wall
for the king to see,
for the prophet to read
and pass along the bad news:
a bulletin of naked mechanics and the Cosmos,
gravity and all that, tear and wear,
erosion and skin bags of bones and blood,
full for a time of action and then still.

Jim E. Lee, blockhead, feels the dance motion,
muscular against inertia,
reaching, arcing, against the pull down,
discomfort over comfort,
pain over sedation—and a fireworks of beauty!

Jim E. Lee puts down one foot and then the other
and moves down the road to the New Jerusalem,
never reached,
and yet reached
in the stepping from here on the way to there,
arrival unimportant,
the pilgrimage steps the city on the hill,
the shining light to the nations,
the sacred pace the holy place.

Jim E. Lee, fool, carries his bag
of shrapnel and mirror shards,
sticking through the burlap,
and walks his haunted house
and walks each of his road's landscapes
and walks the concerto and the pas de deux
and refuses the fetal curl, alive to being born.

Let the Baby Sleep

Steel sharp

I tattoo the
inside of my
skull, blue
on white bone,
and red and
green, the
golden goddess
rising from the
sea—you gotta
love Botticelli—
as nude as the
born baby except
for the wind-
waved hair, and
a naked Achilles
except for the
helmet and arm
brass and sweat
tang, the born
baby knowing
and not knowing
his flaw of
breathing, the
body pulled
behind the
chariot, brittle
pride of golden
mother-huntress,
undefeated
undefeatable
lady of victory,

goddess immune
to born baby
keening for
open door and
face and breast,
born baby holding
close soft cage
cradling steel
sharp rage like
a toxic nest.

That nervous one

He loved that nervous one full,
  even though he was the baby
    she taught bewilderment.
      She got demanded devotion.
        She told him: "Baby, don't cry."

The cloud of every thing

All he knew of stars
in his gray asphalt neighborhood was broken glass.
The two-flat brick Chicago wall was his sacred writ.

    All will be well—all manner of things jagged,
    the mechanism, the empty, filled,
    the shattered made whole.

    All showings are visions. All visions, a blindness.

He ached all over. Never was a time he did not ache.
You can see it in the earliest photos. There,
in that one with the trolley in the background—see?

    All is not yet performed,
    not ended, even the far past.
    All echoes. All ripples on the face of the sea.

He was all shook up. Never settled.
All things must pass unless they don't.
Nervous birdsong by the summer alley.

    All is calm. All is bright. All in all.
    All is story. All hands on deck

He was named All Glory.
He was called Sorrowful Mystery.
He was a hidden prophecy riding the el.
He was a seed on dry concrete, waiting.

    All is said and done. All the way. By all means.
    One size fits all.

He read all the tales of steel and glass.
He studied their parables, pondered their lessons,
made notes in small handwriting in composition books
at a McDonald's table after eating his Egg McMuffin.

Each word burned the page like a fire-tong on the lips.
He was a cloud of incense rising above the street grid.

Never delivered

Package goods

You saw me as the package you delivered.
The box was fine for you,
the brown wrapping, the taping,
the address that said your name so legibly.
You were content.

Why open the package that you delivered
when it was fine as it was, easy to store,
easy to stack with the other packages you delivered?

This package you delivered and the others
could be left in any room and forgotten
until you returned and there they were, packaged.
That was convenient.

The package you delivered and the others
knew nothing else. They had only their place.
They did not disorder.

The package you delivered and the others
understood they were
the brown wrapping and the taping
and the address—yes, the address—
and what was inside was unsettling.
This was understood.

After all, above all, in all,
you who delivered the package and the others
was a package to them, never opened,
never disordered to the air and light
and fearful limitlessness.
Never delivered.

Four percent pantomime

Beethoven's *Symphony #7 In A, Opus 92, Allegretto*, is dread and endurance, deepening in intensity with each new phrase, down into the core. And, for just a few beats, somewhere near the end, I see a ballerina, not leaping, but, with her shoulders wide, striding, step by measured step, as all of us must, to the executioner.

At the Museum of Fine Art, the glazed terra cotta della Robbia Mary holds her baby son with one large hand around his waist and the other over the top of his skull, gripping, with a raw ache, his hair through her fingers, holding for dear life, and, for a glimmer, I see the boy's head move just slightly as if fussed by a bad dream and her lips bend to touch his forehead, as if to kiss away what is to come for her and for him after they return to their pose.

Over my head, the electricity of eight younger bodies cracks from one side of the back yard to the other as the sharp-moved mother arranges the line of food and dishes and utensils on the table and the dutied father is firing the hot dogs, and I am on a blanket, twelve years old, looking deep into the 1961 batting average of Wally Post (.294) and finding, for the briefest moment, a hint of redemption.

The management said to tell the story of my life with a few gestures, like curling into the fetal position and pointing to the lost hope and moving my right thumb across the throat under my innocent chin. Amen.

When she's gone, she's gone.

She's gone like a black page, like a dead tree.
She is an empty womb.

>Let me tell you how I hate
>when she's gone, how I rejoice.

She's gone like the wolf-slashed lamb, a uranium balloon.
She is the cud-chewing land.

>I am on my infant own.

In the other room

Drool chafed your infant chin.
You nervoused her.

You wanted to read the line of ceiling edge,
read the patterned fabric of the big blue chair,
read the sun-shaft dust speck universe,
read his random touch of thumb on left heel,
read her awkward grasp,
read the never-end beyond the window.

No one else looking.

The large dark.

You chewed the brass ashtray
in that Madison Street second-floor flat
while she rearranged furniture,
again and again and again, a clockwork release.

Turned from her as if all fears.

You were chin-thumbed as a joke.

Someone else's bad investment,
wine turned to water,
blinded by mudded spittle,
infested with barbarian demons,
dunked in the leprosy pool—
"What else would you have of me, woman?"

Each wound a caress.

Hearing him and her in the other room.

Absent angel

Mary on the hill,
her dying son,
her aching bones
and flesh, her
flock of his friends
looking to her for
what?

She endured.
The next step
is a step in
any direction.

The thirteen
of us swim in
the suicide of
our brother.
We can't
help but
drink in
the gall.

A sister
sends a
text with
David's
voice like
Abraham's
blooded knife
and no angel
swooping to
the rescue.

Lot's brother

I keep walking and dream of the ocean bottom.

My unhallowed brother candescent with angry song and
furnace flame, keening.

He pulled his own trigger, exploded into darkness.

The bread is broken as the siren interrupts the ceremony.

My resolute brother, doped up with fault from his crib,
whirled so fast he evaporated like so many tears.
His frail voice echoed over the network, final call.

My lost brother's sword and shield
are buried in his backyard where he ended.
When I look in the mirror, I see him.

I am turned into salt.

How

Ash the milk.
Ash the caped-boy hero snapshot.

Ash Blacktop, signboards,
white t-shirt boy.
Ash left hand bunt.
Ash weight circles lift.

    How keen?

Ash altar-boy uniform.
Ash linebacker uniform,
grade school uniform,
marriage-day uniform.

Ash the hair in the furnace,
the toes, the 2 elbows,
the metaled back,
the jaw, the stutter tongue,
the skull, the hole in the skull.

    How dirge?

Mix ash with concrete,
build a short walk through grass
to nowhere,
take the sledge
and slam it down and
again and
again and
again and

again and
again and
again and
again and
again and
fissure cement to sacred handwriting.

Do this in memory.

Lectionary

Utter fox and wolf
words, friend. Speak
swift-foot. Lay waste
the prate. True-breath.

Careen through the
earth-shake, priest.
Girdle fair-gray iron,
sacrament cup. Drink
ill-star vessel. Mercy
the doe-heart votary.

Sand and dust,
daughter. Wed-wife
saint visions. Whirlwind
dust, windstorm sand.
Each a particle.

Forehead-flame song.
Rocky-pilgrim coast. Well-
peopled spirit. Yearn-hope,
pray-petition. Hammer
at arc of weight-fall.

Dawn and thunder
home-return, child;
ox-eye the water. Wine-
dark omen birth. Read
blood feathers, jagged-
fracture bones, empty
church incense. Mist
falls, desire and death.

A reading from the Book of My Brother

Uneat metal apple.
Unask question.
Unfollow directions.
Unlearn lesson.
Unload snake bullets.
Unclimb Tree of Death and Life.
Unfall into temptation.
Unbite.
Unchew barrel.
Untrigger.
Unleave Garden.
Unleave me behind.

Apparitions

(1)

I was told by the old woman of her young
mother walking in Chicago to the railroad
station. Next to her was a woman with a baby girl
asleep on her shoulder who told her: Pray, pray, pray.
The old woman's young mother, heavy with the child
who would be the old woman, sat on a park bench.
Next to her sat Saul Bellow with the Nobel Prize
in his briefcase who told her: That was Our Lady.
She told her daughter who, as an old woman, told me.
Bellow included the scene in a novel left incomplete
at his death in 2005 when I wrote his obituary
for the *Chicago Tribune* twelve years
before the old woman told me the story.

(2)

I told Our Lady my mother
was a water balloon, filled tight with fearful water.
I wanted to throw the balloon with all my strength
against the red-brick wall and see the balloon disintegrate
into shriveled shards of polymer microparticles, and watch
the water drip down the red bricks in the summer sun,
evaporating. She told me her mother was scared of her.

(3)

Our Lady told me she breathed the Holy of Holies.
She was announced. She grew large.
She carried in her gut her God. She bore fruit.
She suffered the slashes of labor and
was sheened in its fluids.
She smelled the baby's skin and crap.
She felt his lips tug and chafe her nipple.
She heard his whimper in his sleep.
She was clothed in the sun and clothed in
old wool for everyday use.
She told me she felt drops of her pierced son's blood
fall on her face and mix with her tears and smear
her cheeks. She was stunned like a Stockyards calf
by brutal holiness.

...ad altare Dei

I offer the purple sash
and the white surplice.

I offer the cold mornings
when snow crunched
and the church was dark
and silent
and an old man
came down the aisle.

I offer the cruets,
and the words at the foot of the altar,
and the priest, heavy with vestments

    Introibo ad altare Dei.

I offer the bells and the cross,
and incense sprinkled on coals.

I offer
the long white tapers
and the flames.

    Ad Deum qui laetificat juventutem meam.

Salome

She danced naked for the Nazi middle-managers
so well that Himmler offered her any thing she
wanted. "Give me the head of Jesus the Baptized."

The Jew was brought in from Gethsemane and sent
up in smoke like so much trash, like a camp fire of
the blonde-haired youth, like the refuse of the race
of masters. Many were caught; some were hanged.
But that didn't bring back the Jew and the six
million others, or the Gypsies, or the POWs, or the
homosexuals, or the partisans, or whoever else got
in the way. There is no vengeance, only sorrow. The
middle-managers were efficient, like the antsy Romans
who broke the legs of the two thieves, like the mother
who got her work done while David crawled his baby
crawl from the front room to the kitchen and became
one of her stories for the rest of his bullet-shortened life.

Did she keep the head in a hat box?

Soon enough

Magnificat

One Cent told Plug Nickel this story
as they walked
down South California Avenue
in the 40-hundreds:

I saw at Burger King,
the one on Lawrence,
the six-year-old eldest
look up at her father
and over at the three younger—
arm out to corral them
from dark shapes, holes, corners,
keeping confusions to herself,
offering thin innocence,
yearning for size
and knowing loneness,
and hearing
as if in the low radio buzz
the sea, lung and gill,
and the sand winds,
Wisdom's whisper.

The problem of human suffering

My moments rosary,
each bead a flighted arrow,
fleshed an edged head.

Can't money aside the bullet,
gleam the path away with polished teeth.

Read the scripture inside the scripture.
Pantomime the silence.

A mansion with many locked rooms.
Turn your face from me.
Gaze not to my affliction.

You are an insect of many eyes,
each slices and does not blink.

The storm never won't oppress.

Howl.

Virgin clowns dance at halftime,
bridegroom quarterback kneels at midfield
to offer his brain to Mother Science
as snow falls and, through green fabric,
pushes up strawberry weed.

Bend back, offer neck to blade,
yearn for angel.

Let the baby sleep.
Soon enough,
she will walk the jagged path,
encased in her fate.

It makes no difference

Patrick crouches
deeper inside his chest shell
as he watches the disciplined boy
kneeling on the marble floor
of the chapel aisle between the seminarian pews
during the Holy Sacrifice of the Mass
and so weightily fearful is the boy that
sweat plops in splash pools beside his knees.

Patrick sweats, too,
heavily, though not to such excess, and,
like Richard, is fearful and laden with his
raw acned existence here in this farm fields school
and a prisoner of the mystery of his insides.

In his hidden warehouse,
stampeding cattle are the pulse and rumble and roar
that cannot be contained and, yet, must be
held back behind the Temple curtain of his face.

Outside McDonald's this morning,
a hooded man cleaning the glass
wobbles on an uneven ladder.

Finding pain

You ask me if,
in writing about my
suicide-brother, I
find peace.

You ask me if
I find a clearing in
the forest where,
amid birdsong, the
sunlight shafts across
my face.

I have found a
jungle on a steep
hill rising to a
mountain and a
mountain top, a
rainstorm and then
blizzard, a whirlwind,
and, at the peak, stingy
air and greedy cold and a
panorama of the Earth spread
for me as
if I were an asthmatic,
hypothermic god, as
if I were again the baby fighting
my way blindly from the dark, as
if I were the
giver of birth, as
if I were the cribbed
infant with no words and a

dread
dream, as
if I were, like all of us, Job
raging out at the Almighty in
the knowledge of death and
the schooling of pain, and
stretching
out to grab
the sorrow-
encrusted
joy
of breathing,
for as
long as
breath
comes.

Real real gone

You are gone, David,
as the page of the book ripped out and
set afire to ash,
as the girl saint tied to the stake and
set afire to ash,
as the sacred offered lambs at the altar of the Temple
set afire to ash,
as the lightninged dry grass
set afire to ash,
as the arsoned restaurant
set afire to ash,
as your self-emptied body sent into the furnace and
set afire to ash.

Distorted by the mother
who sculpted us like trees
and kept her trains running on time,
bent, arc-ed, crook-ed us,
her consort glad it wasn't him.

You are gone
as if you spontaneously combusted over sixty-four years,
set afire to ash.

I am covered in your dust.

Shards

    Ain't I earth's salt?
    Ain't I blue alfalfa fields?
    My light burns through the bushel basket.
    Pearl of great price.

Drive aimed east from airless Hillside
on the bleak text of Eisenhower Expressway—
and my head explodes
from the sacred rifle shot.

Sit before the window,
hear alley crunch,
read mystic lists
of hard-number engineer
who lined paper with Brooklyn Bridge—
and my head explodes
from the sacred rifle shot.

    Blessed cosmic rays, pray for us.
    Lost ways, hear our prayer.
    Misdirected steps, intercede for us.

Stand suited at noonday microphone
at Madison Street and State Street, cosmos center,
speak of the rationalization
of Chicago movement and stasis—
and my head explodes
from the sacred rifle shot.

In my ignorance, in my concupiscence,
in my flexion, in my confusion,
in my will, in my keening,
in my transmission, in my metastasis,
in my wilderness, in my prophecy,
in my ravings, in my contrition,
in my transubstantiation, in my conception.

Look north.
Eat broken bread.
Yearn.

    Keep holy. Keep holy

Shards of my skull
land on the trunk shine
and smear,
shouldered by wind off to pavement,
ground beneath
speed-up tires of the follow car,
embed in concrete pores
with the stew
that, struck by electric sky,
births biology
and the grief of breathing.

    Keep faith.

Sugar Jets

I was six and unclear on the concept.
The commercial, black and white, for Sugar Jets
told me, if I ate a bowl, I would be jet-propelled.

I could see the boy and girl eat Sugar Jets
and fly around the box, jet-propelled.
They were drawings. But a contract was offered,
I thought.

You can see where this is going.

I nagged my mother or maybe my father
—a scary proposition, either way—
to buy Sugar Jets, without saying why.

A box was bought.
I ate a bowl
and went to the back porch, two flights up
from the pavement and lawn below,
looked out over the yard and alley and Blacktop,
a gray pavement playground.

At least I didn't throw myself off.

Instead, I waited for whatever would happen
to jet-propel me
out into the air
and into freedom
and into wonder, maybe a rebirth of wonder.

I am still waiting.

Lament

Take your fingers and
trace the sculpture skin
shards, broken bottles
embedded in wall cement
top. Thieve over and in
for treasure:

my brother,
untriumphed as he felt,
unprotected,
unblossomed.

In middle night, I miss
again high-altitude
Albuquerque basketball
shots, just a game. No
harm, no foul.

You need to picture my
brother raging at my
photograph poems,
stealing his soul,
speaking for him,
poking into the wound
he owned—none
written if, with his
fatal gun, he had not
tunneled his bullet through
my brain and heart and
liver in November snow
-rain on his final porch.

Let the Baby Sleep

I am given flyers for move-
on loss lectures I do not
want to attend. I'll stay
here where my brother is
half alive still. Where I am
alive and know my shots
didn't fall and we lost, but
survived to attend the
museum salsa concert with
all the loose-hip dances,
all the sheen forehead
smiles. I swim survival.

No floating for my brother
and me amid rocks,
rapids of poems. Swim
at own risk.

There is nothing to be
done in the calculus of the
game but to run, sweated,
wearied, behind the arc
and shoot another three
that clanks off the rim at
an odd angle to the other
team, the winning team.
He loved a uniform.

The back door clenched
shut behind my brother as
he stood wobbly behind his
house and raised the metal.

At the baby shower in the
brewery, he would have
asked for milk glass and had
no place to sit and left early.

He would have scrunched
his neck as I do from
some childhood muscle
memory, the way others
smile as they baby-learned
or dance or let their
hips swing loose just
walking a corridor or
a tunnel.

Outside the museum, the
carved head of a giant,
unembodied, eyes in bleak
black stone to uninterrupted
blue high-altitude evening
sky, unsettled and unsettling,
head and sky both, as my
brother and I were, and I
remain.

Swing

Mary Beth and I swing under slow backyard clouds,
singing full-throat grade-school songs,
a moment in a long, dense childhood,
sister and brother, oldest of many.

The mechanism sewn in our skulls
like a blue-ink number
kept all of us focused
on the bouldered uniform-wearer and
the nervoused furniture-arranger.

> I loved that nervous one full,
> even though I was that boy
> she taught bewilderment.
> She got demanded devotion.
>
> She told me: "Baby, don't cry."

My book treasured
self-gone David, another oldest,
pained as he was,

and me and the others,

a romance of children,
tamped down, packed tightly,
like David's head-holed body,
casketed, set afire to ash,
in the oven.

> Cry, baby.

Buried her ashes

Buried her ashes, two years after.
Had to. They told me,
those voices that used to still for her.
They turned, she told them, they went.
We had the plot, right of RODRIGUEZ.
Went along.

Did novena at St. Lucy's,
the stories, rhythms,
the shadows and stained light,
the shine of hard dark wood.
Jesus falls a third time.

After,
walking up to a daughter's house,
grabbed her young son's hair,
threw him to the grass, kept going.
Boy never complained.
I don't.

Nuns recited suffering, salvation.
I have no running sores, lumps, leprosy.
But under skin, black bile.
Uncleanness has scarred my lips,
festered inside.

Didn't want to strip off the uniform.

Why expect better when ashes?
Why ashes? Why without her?
Why the fruit rotted?

Let the Baby Sleep

I smelled the rot, face to pavement.
Knee left stiff. Put up with it.

Put up with those voices.
That boy was too much.
He never complained.
I don't.

Kept it in.

My brother's afflictions and mine

He was a self-contained plague. He
had locust clouds in his brain. I
looked away—from him, from those
two who had no time for me except
to acolyte them. Deuteronomic
abominations get screen clicks, but
the afflictions inflicted on my
brother, quiet, unseen, twisted
him like dislocated branches on
woven living trees and wrenched his
free-will offerings and shaped,
daintily, his self-death—joke-butted
from infanthood, stuttered, a left-
handed cross to bear for mother and
father who had pressing preoccupations:
each other.

My brother tried and learned there was
no answer, no embrace. I looked away,
dodging side-step the steel-bar comedy,
enduring only small bone breaks knit
crooked. My brother's bones—you
understand, it's not the bones of which
I speak—were brutal curled, his tender
back electric pain, his head atwitch, his
feet and hands crushed under lessons he
could not help but listen, he hungered. I
looked 1000 miles away. From them. From
him.

Rage the whirlwind rain.
Face the void.

Workingman's blues #7

Remember that story the
Greeks used to tell about
five runners, each on own
path, with news of Crete—the
one dead of mountain path
fall; another, snakebit; a third,
enemy-spy arrowed; the fourth,
lost, never found; and the fifth,
arriving at the feet of Klemos,
gasping, "West," and dying?

Remember Klemos sending
his own runners east to buy
vineyards and fields near
reaping, and, after bleak
battle across west land,
selling wheat and wine to
victor—Cretans or
Greeks, what matter?

Remember the coda—his
great-grandson's flesh, in
atonement, ripped, slashed,
shredded sun-up, sun-down,
and, in night dark, grown
back pure for violation
again in daylight in price
for Klemos who was, even
then, still planning, far from
final bed, more treasury?

Let us now

Herod's dancer is as much his
victim as the Baptizer.

Understand there is no understanding.

The flesh boy sees Post-it notes on
every wall, telling him his empty-
ness, telling him what he feels isn't.

Look: The creche. She and he
hold the baby still, an embrace-lock.

He is, she tells him, mad at the world.

She chisels the stone of him and scrapes and knocks
away what she disdains, an artist with her mallet,
working against the grain for greater tension, and locks
the work in a lightless room.

Let us now praise her.

That is what she wants.

Enough to be on your way

You disembodied when you had
enough to be on your way.

You disconnected,
discoupling, finally, from the mother ship
and from each of us,
every man jack and dockside sally.

Dispiered as you disappeared
into the tunnel through your brain,
cast off, disshored.

Dissorrowed your soul
with fingerprints on the metal
of the last thing you touched,
your last action
before, empty, you fell as sack of vitals
disvitaled.

You dissinnered yourself who
was more wronged,
disguilted who was pure, stained,
disconvicted who was on the other end of the gun.

I would embrace you now
though you and I learned early
the rule of disembracement,
disbrotherhood, diskinship, dislove.

No one wants to hear this.
Shut up. Ignore it. You're wrong.

Baby, don't cry. I mean it: Don't cry.
Don't disobey.

Those who demanded our care
though we were cribbed—
they took that photo of
you screaming in rage, one,
me looking to forever, two,
both disciplined.
We displeased them.

Dischildrened we were,
adulted.

You disengaged, disgripped, disbreathed
when you had enough to be on your way.

Enough, finally,
distanced yourself.

Dissuffered,
disbirthed,
disconceived.

Steps

Strode Calvary Road
in Maryland and in Kentucky,
in Santa Barbara, Texas and Delaware,
Kansas, Minnesota, Massachusetts.

Strode past churches and cemeteries,
past 7-Elevens and laundromats,
and kept on walking.

The Golgotha steps were mundane
as the Covid air, empty-tang threat,
routine as breathing.

Hitchhiked to Sinai desert,
to Well of Souls,
to Masada shards.
Hitchhiked to wall of tears.
Rolled dice.

George Washington never saw this view:
Capitol, shining shrine on a hill,
blinding as a voting booth.

Drove to my parents' grave,
to my sunset softball catch,
to my brother's walk from Loop.
Drove home.
Lowered blinds.

Photograph of a Saint,
Lisieux's daughter,
dining at the table of sinners.

She was a woman.
She was an arrow in flight.
She was acquainted with infirmity.

Trucked to Mount of Olives,
to Samaritan well,
to Galilee and Bethlehem.
Trucked to Gethsemane.
Closed door.

Walked to the rock and its dome,
to Foundation Stone,
to Abraham and Night Journey.
Walked to prophet foot.
Spun lock.

Rat tracks in snow,
feathers of carcass,
skeleton, a calligraphy of cosmos,
chaos of hunger, life and death,
alpha, omega,
road and hill,
steps.

Let me tell you

Plug Nickel and One Cent
met on museum steps and, inside,
mysticked with blue innocent Della Robbia,
rhythmed the light-shine white
of beyond, above, bright,
orisoned warm-milk fired clay, like flesh,
god-child in supple mother embrace.
Sigh of centuries.

Out straight west, they drove
their wood-paneled station wagon,
out past the 30-hundreds, the 40-hundreds,
nearly to the 52-hundreds
on the table-top Chicago grid,
out to Leamington to meet the gray-pants boy,
sitting on front porch steps, in full view—a
white-red-striped t-shirt buzz-cut good-boy,
out from inside, away, at large,
watching ant-gang heft cornbread crumbles
except this one alone, down sidewalk square
to an insect Promised Land.

He looked up at the two men,
vaguely priestly, vaguely outlawed,
said: "I'm looking to flee captivity
for the sin I don't recall committing."

"We're guilty, too," they said, and
the three walked to afternoon church,
for Stations of the Cross,
flaming altar candles, up, reaching always up,

echoes, shuffling, Latin abracadabras,
plainsong up, incense up from censer,
from burning coal, straining up,
cloud of unknowing, cloud of Mount Sinai,
cloud of breathing and not breathing.

After Amen, the three split up
and went home by a different path.

About the Author

Photograph of author by Steve Kagan
Sugar Jets by General Mills

Patrick T. Reardon is the author of twelve books, including the poetry collections *Requiem for David*, *Darkness on the Face of the Deep* and *The Lost Tribes*. His memoir in prose poems *Puddin': The Autobiography of a Baby* was published by Third World Press with an introduction by Haki Madhubuti. It has been described by *Mindbender Review of Books* as "quite possibly the most ingeniously imagined memoir by any writer". His poetry collection *Salt of the Earth: Doubts and Faith* is forthcoming from Kelsay Books.

For 32 years, Reardon was a *Chicago Tribune* reporter, specializing in urban affairs. In 2020, his non-fiction history book *The Loop: The "L" Tracks That Shaped and Saved Chicago* was published by Southern Illinois University Press.

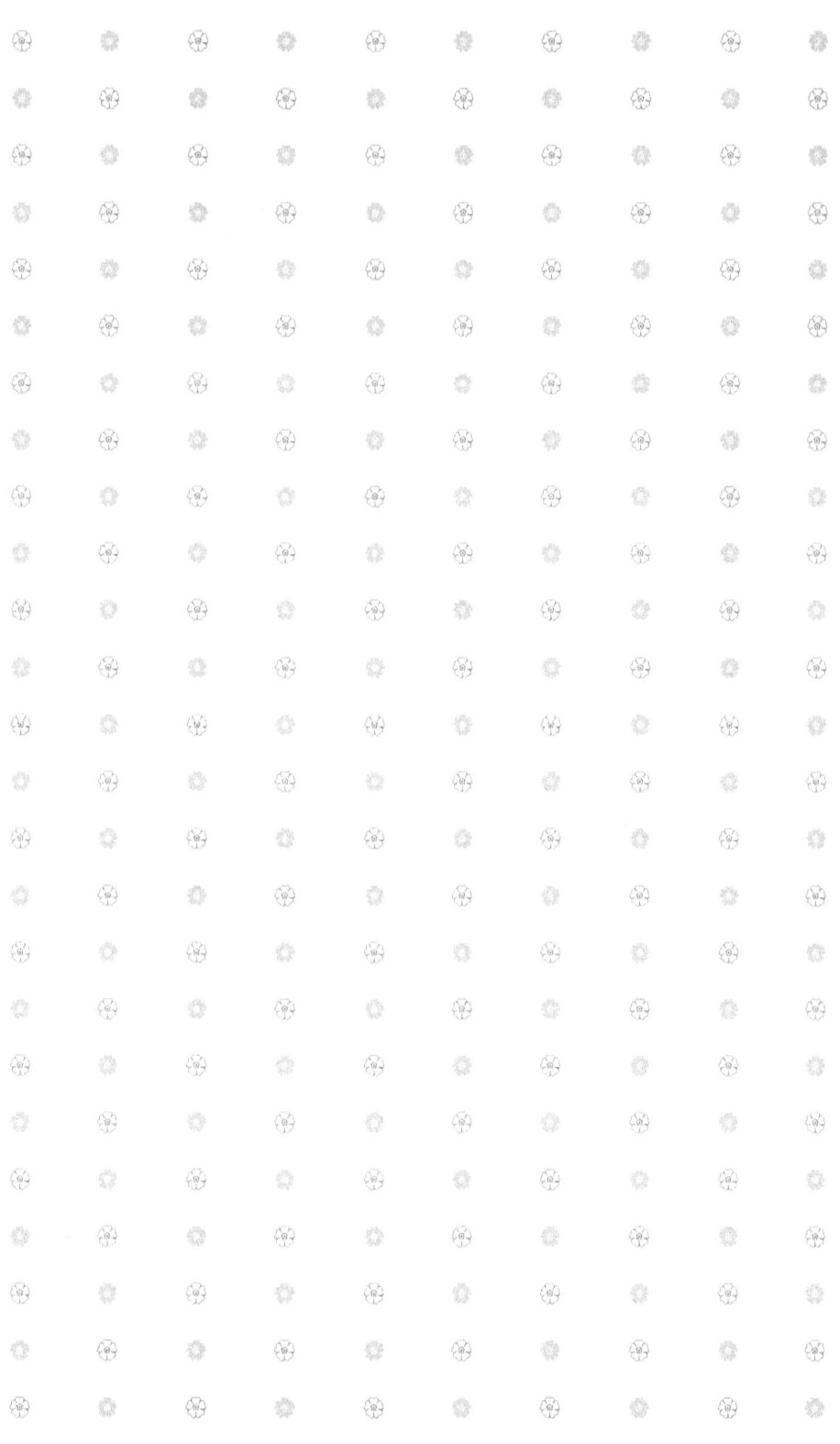

www.ingramcontent.com/pod-product-compliance
Lightning Source LLC
Chambersburg PA
CBHW030302010526
44107CB00053B/1784